GARDENING BY DESIGN

WARD·LOCK

THE

EVENING GARDEN

PETER McHOY

D1384608

Distributed by
STERLING PUBLISHING CO., INC.
387 Park Avenue South
New York, N. Y. 10016-8810

GARDENING BY DESIGN

WARD · LOCK

THE
EVENING GARDEN

PETER McHOY

WARD LOCK

ACKNOWLEDGEMENTS

The publishers are grateful to the following for granting permission
to reproduce the following colour photographs: the author (pp. 31,
50, 58, 59, 62 & 63); and Hozelock – A.S.L. Ltd. (pp. 42, 43, 54 &
66). The photographs on pp. 14, 15, 18, 19, 22, 23, 26, 27, 30, 34, 35,
38, 39, 46, 47, 51, 55, 67, 70 & 71 were taken by Bob Challinor. The
publishers are also grateful to Hozelock – A.S.L. Ltd. for supplying
the Hi-Light lamps shown in the photographs on pp. 14 and 15.

All the line drawings were drawn by Nils Solberg.

First published 1988 by Ward Lock
Villiers House, 41-47 Strand, London WC2N 5JE

First paperback edition 1991
A Cassell imprint
© Ward Lock Ltd 1988, 1991

House editor Denis Ingram
Text set in Bembo
by TJB Photosetting Ltd, South Witham, Lincolnshire

Printed and bound by Graficromo s.a., Cordoba, Spain

British Library Cataloguing in Publication Data
McHoy, Peter, 1941–
    The evening garden.———Gardening by design)
    1. Gardens—Great Britain—Design
    2. Gardening—Great Britain
    I. Title   II. Series
    712′6′0941   SB472.32.G7
    ISBN 0-7063-6965-3

CONTENTS

PREFACE

If you are one of those gardeners with time to enjoy your hobby during the day, the chances are you usually regard dusk as the time to pack up and go indoors; and if you are out at work during the day, for much of the year you will be arriving home when it is simply too dark to enjoy the garden. So often the evening is a time of missed opportunities in the garden: a time when gardens are ignored rather than enjoyed. It doesn't have to be that way of course, as anyone who has learnt to make the best of the twilight hours will testify. You too can discover the magic that can transform a garden into a place of light and beauty after dark.

There are enormous possibilities that an evening garden can bring. Planning at least parts of your garden with evening in mind will certainly extend the hours of pleasure that you can derive from it, and it can actually help to give you a new lifestyle.

Using the garden in the evening has to be for pure enjoyment. It is *not* a time for working in your garden, but a time for relaxation and enjoyment. Even in the depths of winter, you can enjoy viewing it from indoors by the clever use of garden lighting.

Evening gardens are not simply to be enjoyed for a few brief months in summer. With careful positioning and illumination it is possible to look out onto it from the house, perhaps through French windows or patio doors. You won't be able to enjoy the distinctive fragrance that comes with a well-planned evening garden in summer, but indoors you will at least be able to enjoy the visual delights from the comfort of your home.

Creating an evening garden does not necessarily involve redesigning your whole garden, or even spending much money. It may only mean modifying the patio and perhaps the area around it, or redesigning a small corner of the garden for evening use. A small, cosy corner planned for evening relaxation may be more effective than a large garden with extensive lighting that looks impressive initially but does not encourage you to sit, relax, and reflect.

A garden that is cared for demands a lot of attention. It makes sense to get the best from it by extending its use into the evening too.

P. McH.

1

ILLUMINATION AND INSPIRATION

The garden can be at its most dramatic and beautiful at twilight when the garden lights have been turned on and while there is still enough natural light to see other features and detail in the background. Quite ordinary plants, if they are tall enough, can very often seem strangely unreal and exciting viewed against a full moon.

Twilight is a fleeting moment, of course, and although it is there to be savoured, it is only a moment in the kaleidoscope of delights in the evening garden. Even the ordinary can be transformed by a few wisely chosen and carefully positioned lights. But there is more to an evening garden than lights alone. It is necessary to choose plants or features that look good illuminated, and of course to make the best of those plants that are at their most fragrant at night.

A conservatory will provide even more scope. You will be able to use it for evening relaxation and entertainment long before it is comfortable to sit outside in the evenings … and of course it will extend the season too.

Having illuminated the garden for effect, it makes sense to *use* it as much as possible in the evenings. A stroll around the fragrant flower beds, a moment's pause to admire an illuminated cascade, perhaps admire the striking profile of an ornament picked out in a spotlight, offers pleasant but limited enjoyment. It is much more fun to share your garden with others,

and Chapter Five contains plenty of ideas for outdoor entertainment.

WHAT'S INVOLVED

It's not difficult to spend a lot of money on garden lighting if your plans are very ambitious, but planning part of your garden for the evening does not have to be an expensive exercise. If you have a large garden, you'll probably want only part of it for evening use (with maybe a spotlight or two on key features further away); and if your garden is no bigger than most of those found on modern housing estates, you will be able to achieve quite striking results for a very modest outlay.

It is possible to buy quite effective garden lighting for little more than, say, a couple of choice shrubs, but equally you can pay ten times this amount for a single lamp if you want something more elegant and individual.

Some outdoor lighting can be potentially dangerous unless properly installed by a competent electrician, but there are plenty of low-voltage systems around that you can install perfectly safely yourself, both quickly and easily. In fact you can bring them home from the shop and usually have them operating in the garden within an hour.

PRACTICAL OR PRETTY

There are highly practical as well as decorative reasons for using garden lights. For example, lighting steps (Fig. 1), patios and door areas (Fig. 2) helps to prevent accidents; lights by the drive make it safer for drivers and pedestrians; and porch and wall lights can help security too.

Lights are sometimes used for their security value alone, being timed to come on while you are out or perhaps away on holiday, or being triggered to flood-light part of the building or garden when anyone passes through an invisible ray. These automatically triggered systems need careful siting and adjustment to prevent them from flashing on unexpectedly every time a cat walks along your garden wall.

This book is about the decorative use of garden lights, not house and garden security, but it makes sense if you can combine the two (Fig 3). Lighting around the house and garden, especially the front garden, can be a deterrent to burglars, who tend to prefer the shadows of night.

Time-switches

Time-switches are a good solution if you are in the habit of using your garden lighting regularly but would otherwise not use it when you are away. There are also light-sensitive switches available that will turn on the lighting when the sun goes down. It makes sense to have porch lights so that you can identify visitors, and it's wise to illuminate any potential hazards such as steps. This kind of lighting can be fairly plain and functional, but it doesn't have to be.

Fig. 1 Low-level lighting is particularly effective for steps that are likely to be used after dark, such as on a patio used for evening entertainment.

Fig. 2 A porch light can be welcoming to visitors and a deterrent to burglars. If security is an important consideration, a wide beam is likely to be the most effective.

Fig. 3 Used imaginatively, lights can enhance the garden and contribute to safety. Here concealed overhead lights illuminate a path while bringing to life a dark corner of the garden.

Bulkheads

The simplest form of lighting for paths, patios and porches are the 'light bricks' or 'bulkhead' fittings. These are usually square or oval, often with some wire protection to reduce the risk damage from knocks. You can get them from most lighting shops and some large general stores, unlike many of the more decorative garden lights, which are usually sold by garden shops and more specialist retailers.

Bulkhead fittings are not usually particularly elegant (although some of the round wall lights are attractive). However they are cheap and when they are switched on, you do not normally see the light source anyway — what you see is what is illuminated and the fitting will probably be invisible.

Lanterns

Post lanterns are suitable for entrance drives but, like most permanent fixtures not actually attached to the wall of the house or outbuilding, you will need permanent power supplied probably through conduit or armoured cable.

Some lanterns are designed for mounting on a low wall, others are on their own bollards. Most of them are attractive as well as practical and functional.

OVERALL DESIGN

The patio is usually thought of as a place of pleasure rather than danger, but it is no use having decorative lighting if the patio becomes a place of potential hazards because the lighting is inadequate from a functional viewpoint.

Lighting should always be adequate around the barbecue, where there is the activity of preparing a meal. Steps or changes of level must also be adequately illuminated in such spots, and dark shadows avoided.

With the exception of party or festoon lights, which are intended as pure decoration, most garden lights will make the garden a safer place by night as well as a prettier one.

Lighting is best regarded as a decorative adjunct to the overall garden design, rather than an end in itself. Mounting a couple of lanterns on the gate posts and bathing the patio with light from a powerful floodlamp does not make an evening garden. Lighting can be subtle, with a low hidden lamp bringing a foliage shrub to life with dancing shadows as the leaves move in the breeze; tasteful with an ornament picked out in its niche in a dark, creeper-clad wall; or dramatic as a tree is emphasized against the dark skyline. Whatever you choose, make sure it forms part of an overall design, making the garden a place to use in the evening.

2

PATIO AND CONSERVATORY

The patio is usually associated with daytime use; the word brings to mind images of sunny, sultry summer days. But it is also the natural focal point for an evening garden. With a sensible choice of lighting (Fig 4), many activities can be extended into the evening. In fact it is here that much of your evening entertaining will probably take place, and if you want to treat your patio very much as an extension of the home it's the place that you will want to spend many of your evenings.

THE RIGHT POSITION

Although most patios are built next to the house, there is no reason why it should not be at the end of the garden, or anywhere else that gives you a good view of the garden, adequate privacy, and plenty of shelter in a sunny position.

If there is a power supply nearby, perhaps in a greenhouse, it may be less expensive than you think to install lighting there. However, in the absence of an existing power point, it will be less expensive, and more convenient, to have the patio close to the main building if you plan to use it in the evening. You will be able to use party lights, and many of the temporary outdoor patio lights, without a lot of trailing cable or the need for long extension and potentially hazardous leads. Permanent lights can be fixed to the house wall relatively inexpensively, and other lights needing permanent wiring should be less expensive to install

because of the shorter runs of cable required, and of course less ground excavation will be necessary.

DESIGNING A PATIO

If you are planning a patio from scratch, there are a few basic rules to bear in mind.

You will probably want to use it by day as well as in the evening, so it needs to be in a sunny position, and sheltered from winds (important during the day, even more so at night when there's a chill in the air). This may not be conveniently outside the French windows or sliding doors, but it may be possible to have it slightly to one side of the house with a small amount of linking paving.

Make a note of the prevailing wind direction (you will already know from experience whether there is a wind funnelling effect caused by the proximity of other buildings).

Screening

In any case you will need to provide some shelter if the patio is to have a cosy, intimate, and well designed appearance. Privacy is important too, especially where houses are close together and the garden is easily overlooked by neighbours. If you feel overlooked during the day, you will be even more conscious of the lack of privacy after dark. With the lights on, the patio will be illuminated like a stage. The lights will attract attention, and it is inevitable that people on the patio will become part of the spectacle.

It is also important that lights do not shine into neighbours' houses, which is less likely to be a problem with proper screening and careful positioning of the lights.

Shelter can be provided by plants or by a more solid structure. Living screens take longer to become effective, but in many cases they are better at filtering the wind than solid structures, which can cause eddies and undesirable turbulence.

It is tempting to plant fast-growing conifers such as Leyland cypress (× *Cupressocyparis leylandii*), but anything that grows that fast is unlikely to stop when it reaches the height that you want. They also need regular trimming and can look dark and oppressive. Better to consider evergreen shrubs if there is enough space, or to choose something like tall bamboos that will form a thicket of known height – and look really good as a background for so many other features. Bamboos, with their Oriental connotations, have just the right amount of 'atmosphere' for an illuminated garden.

Ordinary timber fencing looks somehow too commonplace and crude for the patio, but a slatted fence of the 'hit and miss' type (with horizontal bars either side of substantial uprights) combines privacy with an effective windbreak and a strong sense of design.

Screen (pierced) block walls can look good, especially if you are providing just localized screening around the patio itself, but try planting plenty of evergreen shrubs in front of it for more privacy and interest.

Patio overheads are useful in any case because they give the area a more enclosed and intimate effect, but if you are overlooked by neighbours' upstairs windows there's the added benefit of screening from above.

It's easy to place too much emphasis on an overhead. Let climbers provide most of the canopy. Filling it in with plastic sheeting of various types is not without drawbacks. Leaves and debris can soon make it look dirty, and the noise of heavy rain on it can be particularly distracting.

Instead use a blind or awning that you can pull out when you need it. This will provide welcome shade during bright days, and the necessary shelter to continue your barbecue if it starts to rain. At the same time, being made of a material that you cannot see through, it will provide privacy and reduce the amount of light thrown upwards that could annoy your neighbours.

Canvas screens around the end of a patio can be useful too, perhaps bridging the gap between a low wall and overhead beams. These can be removed when not required, and put up again when you need shelter from sun or wind. They also might be useful in preventing stray light from annoying your neighbours.

Paving

A patio should be more than a simple area of paving. To achieve a designed and sophisticated look, it should incorporate features like raised beds, perhaps a built-in seat (possibly a built-in barbecue too), and perhaps a change of level.

The paving itself will set the tone of the patio, so try to avoid plain rectangular paving slabs parallel to the house. Consider alternatives such as bricks or pavers, or some of the more decorative paving blocks. Try setting them at an angle to the house, especially if the patio is situated at a corner of the building.

The larger the patio, the more necessary it is to provide a change of texture. Don't be afraid to mix materials: railways sleepers and bricks; paving slabs and clay pavers or bricks; cobbles and paving slabs. But don't get carried away: if you mix more than three, there is a risk of it looking fussy rather than effective.

A change of level can be provided by low raised beds; but a few shallow steps to another level of paving can be particularly impressive. Level changes do not have to be steep, but they do have to be properly illuminated for night use.

If you are fortunate enough to have a side wall available so that the patio can be built with walls on two sides, try painting the wall with a white masonry paint

a

Fig. 4 If you have a conservatory, it's a good idea to link it with a patio so that home and garden merge. When you entertain, friends can drift easily between patio and conservatory – especially useful if the weather becomes cold or unsettled in the evening. Such an arrangement is successful both by day (*a*) and by evening (*b*).

It is often more effective to illuminate a small but interesting corner of the garden than to floodlight a large area.

Lamps do not have to be ornate to be effective; something simple can be successful.

(or any light colour that might harmonize the colour scheme in any adjoining room). It will reflect light and make everything less gloomy after dark or on dull days.

Plants for the patio

If raised beds are not a practical proposition (or even if they are), try also to use plenty of tubs and other substantial containers. A few large tubs with shrubs or other big plants will do more to give the patio character than lots of window-boxes and baskets with seasonal bedding – though these are necessary to provide pockets of colour that may otherwise be missing.

The best patios have plenty of planting space at ground level. Too much hard landscaping without the accompanying planting areas to soften the outline will look harsh and uninspirational. At the very least leave out some paving slabs to plant into, but better still design proper planting areas into the scheme.

For evening use you need lots of these beds for fragrant shrubs and annuals, and for plants with a strong shape and form to be picked out with spotlights.

If you have to build some raised beds or higher walls, it's worth trying to incorporate a position for a small but tasteful ornament, such as a small bust. This will make a good focal point during the day, and can look dramatic picked out by a spotlight in the evening.

PRACTICAL LIGHTING

A patio may not be a safe place after dark, especially one with different levels, and maybe an overhead with suspended hanging baskets. Make sure all the danger areas are illuminated. Steps and changes of level are a priority, and in this respect a light source at ground level is more practical than high illumination. However, beware of flooding the whole area with light, which can look too harsh and will spoil the effect of more decorative lighting.

It may be possible to have low lights that on the one hand illuminate part of a bed or just a small group of plants, and on the other cast enough low light to show up the edge of the level change. For a flight of steps, it is worth looking for fittings that can be recessed into the sides of the steps: discreet, simple, and very effective.

Access points and possible overhead obstacles, such as hanging containers, also need adequate, if discreet, lighting. It is tempting to use too much overhead lighting (a bulkhead light on the wall of the house is very efficient, but the effect is functional rather than dramatic), but flooding the area with too much brilliance will detract from the atmosphere of an intimate garden. Far better to choose small low-powered lights at strategic points to create localized pools of light. A wall-mounted bulkhead light will be useful when you want to work or clear up, or simply for normal security, but change to something more subtle when your guests arrive.

LIGHTING FOR BARBECUES

These days a barbecue is an almost essential part of outdoor living, and an integral part of many patios. However, never lose sight of the fact that this is a work area, and just as you would not think of preparing a meal over a hot surface in the kitchen unless the light was adequate, so you should apply the same standards in the garden when cooking.

The work area – including storage areas – and all the utensils that you need, should be well illuminated. This is not to say you should stand in a pool of light and behave like a television chef; a couple of low-powered spotlights, perhaps wall-mounted, directed onto the working surface is all that is necessary. As spotlights usually have a beam that can be adjusted, when the cooking is done you can always redirect them onto some other feature, such as an ornament that you want to highlight, or simply a group of plants.

CHOOSING LIGHTING

The choice of lighting should respect the style of architecture of the house. Imitation coach lamps can look totally incongruous against a 1940s house; a pseudo-Victorian lamp standard can look pretentious against a modern house with a tiny garden. There are plenty of styles available — it is just a matter of looking through catalogues or visiting lighting retailers to find something that you like and which is still in keeping with the style of the house and garden.

CONSERVATORIES

Good conservatories are not cheap, so it makes sense to get as much use from them as possible. Although the conservatory is a plant room as well as a people room, it need not be simply somewhere that you sit during the day. In fact on a hot summer's day it may be too warm for comfort, and the cool of the evening is an ideal time to enjoy the freshness provided by an abundance of plants.

A sun-room with the emphasis on furniture rather than plants, may already be fitted out with domestic lighting, perhaps fluorescent tubes, but the use of spotlights – rail-mounted with plenty of scope for adjustment to highlight different plants – will add much to the atmosphere and will make the very best of relatively few plants.

However, a proper conservatory will have many more plants and a generally damp, humid atmosphere that is totally unsuitable for ordinary domestic light fittings. In many ways it is like a greenhouse, and as such you should use waterproof equipment that will also resist the ravages of damp and humidity.

CONSERVATORY LIGHTING

Overhead lighting is likely to be the most practical, not only because it is less likely to be splashed when you water, but also because low-level lighting is unlikely to show plants on benches to their best advantage.

The level of lighting is not likely to have much effect on the growth of the plants, as even the fluorescent tubes intended to stimulate plant growth need to be very close to the plants. However, it may be worth using growth lights above those plants that are likely to respond particularly well to additional light, such as African violets (saintpaulias). For this to be really effective, you need lights that produce energy at the right part of the spectrum for growth. If you want to use fluorescent tubes, try tropical fish shops: the lamps used for aquariums are also suitable for plant growth and flowering, and they are available with fittings that can be used in a damp, humid atmosphere.

Lamps are available that look like ordinary domestic spotlights (with bayonet or screw fittings) that are balanced for plant growth, and these are ideal for illuminating a small group of plants. These also have to be very close to the plants to have a beneficial effect on growth; and unlike fluorescent lights produce a fair amount of heat.

Where most of the plants are grown in borders or in pots at ground level, a combination of overall fluorescent lighting and spotlights on individual plants or groups of plants will provide the best combination. Make sure reflectors direct the light downwards; this not only makes more efficient use of the available light but also reduces the risk of it annoying neighbours. If you have blinds, used for shading the conservatory in summer, it might be worth using these at night too.

If the plants are arranged at floor level, try grouping some of them around an ornament or tasteful statue as a focal point, and illuminate this with a spotlight.

If you have a conservatory, it is a good idea to link this with a patio, so that both become an integrated extension of the home.

A quite ordinary garden scene like this can be transformed in the evening with careful illumination (see photograph opposite).

Relatively low powered spotlights are all that's needed to make a focal point of quite ordinary plants.

3

ORNAMENTS AND FOCAL POINTS

As evening falls, plants and features that were focal points during the day can simply disappear into pools of darkness. It is therefore necessary to create new centres of interest focal points that will lead the eye to a definite part of the garden (Fig. 5).

Sometimes it is merely a matter of illuminating an existing focal point, such as an ornament; but you may have to highlight a feature that is simply part of the background planting during the day. A spotlight on a white-barked silver birch towards the end of the garden, or a spiky yucca at the front of the border, may be all that is needed to lead the eye to an attractive feature.

The same principles apply even in a small garden or a courtyard. Maybe there is a fountain that you can illuminate, or a small wall plaque; the focal point need not be large, nor the light powerful, but an evening garden requires a sense of design as much as a daytime garden. Stringing out a few party lights around the patio may be adequate for the occasional party, but it will not transform it into a place to be proud of.

FEATURING PLANTS

It is worth illuminating groups of plants that look good together where they form a compact arrangement, but generally it is the small, compact plants, perhaps near the edge of a path or part of the patio, that are most effective. It is easy to make these look especially attractive in the evening with small lamps that cast the beam downwards (Fig. 6).

Groupings of small plants will *not* act as a satisfactory focal point. You will need something big and bold, or at least with a striking outline. A large yucca with its stiff spike of large white flowers will take the eye more than any ordinary border plants or shrubs. Other useful plants are suggested in Chapter Four.

Trees can be the boldest plants to illuminate, but they also need the most care – it is too easy to make it all look municipal. Floodlighting that illuminates the canopy of foliage from beneath also can be overpowering in a garden setting, and the amount of stray light generated can be particularly distracting for neighbours. Remember, too, that trees which look pretty in leaf may be unattractive during the winter months.

If you do want to illuminate a tree, choose one with an interesting outline. Many weeping trees are suitable, from a large weeping willow (provided the setting is large enough) to small trees like the silver willow-leaved pear (*Pyrus salicifolia* 'Pendula').

FLOODLIGHT OR SPOTLIGHT?

Garden lighting needs to orchestrated if it's not to be either prosaic, monotonous or garish. Brightness and contrasts will accentuate modelling and form, and produce a visual texture that is unique to the evening garden.

Fig. 5 Pools of light that pick out interesting features are better at creating 'atmosphere', and will usually be more effective than bathing the whole patio with a strong floodlight.

Fig. 6 Flower beds with low plants such as summer bedding are often best illuminated by low lights that cast the beams downwards in a relatively narrow area over the beds.

The beauty of this rose garden would normally be wasted after dark, but it doesn't have to be (see photograph opposite).

A rose garden lends itself to evening use – the roses look good and the fragrance can seem especially potent.

Trees can be illuminated effectively by projecting the light vertically up into the foliage, although it is important to ensure that stray light does not annoy neighbours. If the light is thrown onto the trees from a floodlight placed some distance away, this can be difficult to avoid, but a 100 or 150 watt PAR38 internal reflector lamp concealed close to the trunk, should combine effective illumination with the minimum of annoyance. If there is no suitable position to mount a lamp at the base of the tree, it may be possible to clamp one to a stout low branch. Generally light thrown upwards like this only works well with trees that have a loose branch structure. With a thick, dense head of foliage, front lighting may be the only satisfactory solution.

Fig. 7 Lights that are pretty after dark may have fittings that look far from attractive in daylight. Floodlights can often be masked by dwarf shrubs.

Often small trees with a delicate tracery of branches can look dramatic lit from the back, the branches showing up as a silhouette. Trees like the corkscrew willow (*Salix matsudana* 'Tortuosa') look pretty even in winter when the twisted and contorted branches are silhouetted against the sky or back lighting.

GENERAL POINTERS

With the exception of some of the decorative lamps that are intended to be a feature in their own right, the fittings are best hidden from view. By day functional lamps can detract from the beauty of the beds and borders, and even in the evening the lighting is often less effective if you can actually see the source. With a little ingenuity they can be screened with shrubs (Fig. 7), low-growing plants, or even rocks.

Light *colour* is crucially important to the overall effect. Coloured lenses can create a wonderful 'atmosphere', but the plants will not look real.

FLOWER BEDS

Some lights actually have a beneficial effect on flowering, but it has to be at fairly close quarters and for fairly prolonged periods to have a significant effect.

The subtle hues of many flowers are best reflected by tungsten filament or 'white', 'daylight' or 'warm white' fluorescent lamps. These are sometimes used in troughs or mushroom lamps supported on posts that you can insert into the flower beds. These cast the light downwards, and provided you use enough to illuminate the whole bed it is a beautiful and striking way to get the best from colourful summer bedding. You might even find that they come into flower that bit earlier too.

Side lighting, perhaps attached to an adjacent wall or tree, can be used (Fig. 8). But it is often difficult to avoid light spill that can result in a discomforting glare.

Fig. 8 Thoughtlessly placed lights can annoy neighbours, but by directing beams downwards the result can often be as effective without stray light becoming a nuisance.

STATUES AND ORNAMENTS

If an ornament works well during the day as a focal point, it will probably be effective at night too – but choose just one to illuminate (or possibly two provided they are not both in view at the same time), otherwise one will detract from the other.

Take into account the effect of shadows. The shadows cast can add a sense of drama. A free-standing ornament with a strong outline, or even a bust on a plinth, will cast an interesting long or short shadow, depending on the angle and height of the lamp.

Ornaments are useful for bringing a sense of purpose to, say, an otherwise dull wall, or to an expanse of green hedge. In this case the shadows will merge with the background anyway, and it is usually most effective

A house of character is worth showing off in the evening, but the lamps needn't intrude on the daytime view.

Lighting near the house can improve security, and an attractive house can itself become a focal point.

to pick out the features in a comparatively narrow beam of light so that it is highlighted against the dark background where the shadows merge.

Vases and urns can be illuminated in this way, but they are seldom as effective as statues or figures.

Sculptures and ornaments made of a dark material such as bronze are best seen in silhouette – either by moonlight or viewed against the warm glow of a lower-powered back light. If the material is a pale stone, try to use front lighting. If the light projects downwards, perhaps from a pillar, wall, or tree, an effect similar to daylight can be achieved. For a bust, however, a narrow spotlight may be more dramatic.

If there is no alternative to a ground-mounted light, don't place it too close to the figure, nor immediately beneath it, otherwise the shadows will be too heavy and harsh. If figures are to look right there must be a degree of shadow and detailing, and this may demand a fairly soft light, perhaps slightly to one side to provide the necessary contrast.

THE WATER GARDEN

Water can be used to provide a sense of calm and tranquillity, with other lights simply reflecting on a still surface, or it can create a sense of gaiety and fun with moving water acting as reflectors and refractors so that it sparkles with a jewel-like brilliance.

Ponds provide hours of pleasure at any time, and this need not end as the light fades. Water and lighting can combine to provide that wonderful combination of light and sound if you have a cascade or fountain that can be illuminated. Even with still water there is the bonus of reflections that sparkle where the water ripples in a slight breeze.

The potential of water and lights is enormous, but it is also easy to get it wrong. Too many lights, too many colours, and it can look garish. If the output of underwater lamps is inadequate, the result will be disappointing, especially once they have become covered with a layer of algae.

Moving water looks best picked out in a beam of light (Figs. 9a and b), as it can create shimmering rainbows of dancing light. Floating lamps can be used, perhaps around a fountain, but they have no attraction during the day. As with all garden lighting, it is the light itself that you want to see, not the light fitting.

It will cost more, but a self-contained illuminated fountain is a visually more acceptable approach to underwater lighting. For a plain but tasteful display in a formal or classical setting, a plain or amber lamp is the best choice, but colour changing units are available that rotate colours such as green, red, and blue to give a fairyland effect if you want more of a party atmosphere.

If a party atmosphere is required, some of the underwater floodlamps with interchangeable filters of various colours will give an unreal, almost spooky, light.

Ordinary garden spotlights, well camouflaged amongst the surrounding plants, can be striking in their simplicity. They will bring the dancing jets of a fountain or a bubbling cascade to life as effectively as any underwater light. In winter too, when fountain and cascades will be turned off and the still water can look chilly and uninviting, the lamps can be used to illuminate other features.

If there's a rock garden or other feature behind the pond, pick out plants here too. If coloured lights are used for the pond itself, try red lights and green lights among the rocks or plants behind. This is one case where the unnatural effect of some colours produce a very pretty, if strange, effect with both lights and plants reflected in the water.

Specialist firms can supply a range of fountains that change through an elaborate series of spray patterns with lights that change colour too, but these belong more in a discotheque or a hotel foyer than in a garden.

A single jet of water is enough to break the silence of a still night – try using the narrow beam of a spotlight to highlight the jet as it moves across the water, so that the light rays pass along or through the jet of water.

Sprays of water – perhaps from a fountain – generally need a wide beam, and a cascade is often best back-lit by a concealed light so that it appears as a brilliant

Fig. 9 At night a jet of water is often best illuminated by a beam of light that intersects the jet (a). Upright fountains are generally best illuminated from beneath (b).

sheet of water standing out from the surrounding darkness.

PATIO LAMPS

All kinds of lighting equipment can be used on the patio, of course, and a well designed patio may contain a mixture of several different types.

There are, however, what some manufacturers loosely term 'patio lights'. Many of these, though weatherproof, are intended for temporary use (perhaps for an evening party), being connected to the power supply indoors through, say, an open window or door. Some of these use ordinary domestic light bulbs, though of course these are of necessity protected by a stout globe or some other device so that the bulb does not come into contact with drops of rain for instance.

Lights of this type are excellent for their purpose – they will cast light around a sitting area, near the work area by the barbecue, or illuminate, say, a table where food is being served. They provide light to see by and to stand and chat by ... and they can be quite ornamental too. Many of them are hardly the most elegant lamps by day, but as they are easily portable there is no problem in bringing them out for the occasion and storing them between 'events'.

Outdoor party lights, and what some manufacturers describe as 'barbecue' lights, are discussed in Chapter Five, as most of these are also intended for occasional use. Some of them can be left in position permanently with perfect safety, the wire being taken through the wall to a convenient power supply indoors. They all have waterproof fittings, like the lights used for outdoor illuminations.

The problem about fixing them up outdoors permanently is that they can make your garden look somewhat like a park with coloured lamps strung through trees. It may be fine for Christmas or some other festive occasion, but otherwise they are probably best reserved for those party evenings.

Even if porch lights are primarily practical, adding a few well-planted containers can create a really striking effect.

A welcome at the door. This simple light and a hanging basket give visitors a cheery welcome.

REPRODUCTION LAMPS

There are firms that make elegant reproduction Victorian British lamp-posts, and there may be similar firms in other countries who specialize in 'period' lamp-posts. The most logical place for any of these is by a front drive, but if your garden doesn't possess any-thing as grand as a drive, there are still opportunities for using an ornate lamp-post near, say, a corner of the house. Carefully positioned it can become a focal point by day and a practical light by night, perhaps illuminating a path to the front or back door.

Old-fashioned porch lamps and coach lamps for fixing to gateposts are much less expensive, often not as well made, but nevertheless welcoming to the visitor. Some of these are multi-coloured, and can look pretentious if too many are used.

4

PLANTING FOR EFFECT

No amount of clever hard landscaping, ornaments, or sophisticated lighting, can make a good garden unless it also contains the right plants.

Planting for the evening does not mean an uninteresting garden during the daytime. Most of the plants mentioned in this chapter are good general garden plants anyway. They simply have the bonus of being attractive by night too – whether by fragrance or outline. Just a few, such as night scented stocks, come into their own once darkness falls and are not particularly attractive during the day.

ARCHITECTURAL SHAPE

Once light begins to fade, shades of green become dull and merge into a monotone, and flowers that are attractive by day because of their vivid colour may lose their impact long before darkness falls. Subtle variegation may almost disappear, and even in artificial light may lack appeal.

Shape and form can be as important as colour and flower. Plants that have a distinctive profile will stand out in the evening whether silhouetted against the full moon or bathed with light. A selection of suitable plants is given below, but avoid planting more than a few of them together in one spot – spread them around the garden so that they provide height and shape in different spots, rather than concentrated in one area. Like focal points they can be overdone – too many within eyeshot at once will fight for attention and the impact may be lost. Placed carefully and strategically you will not need many of them. And too many, at the expense of fill-in border plants, shrubs or bedding, will create a garden that lacks daytime appeal.

YUCCAS

The yuccas have to be included because they have such a distinctive profile the year round with their big rosettes of evergreen sword-like leaves, and when they flower the huge stiff spikes of big pure white flowers stand out very well in the evening light. Whether viewed against a skyline in fading light or picked out by a spotlight, a yucca in bloom can hardly fail to impress. It has a rather exotic appearance that separates it from most hardy shrubs.

The yuccas that we grow in gardens are in fact very hardy, and not difficult to grow, although they prefer a hot, dry position in full sun. *Y. gloriosa* (Adam's needle) is the one to grow where you want a yucca with a stout stem to about 1.8 m (6 ft) or so, to give you height. But be warned if you have small children: it has spine-tipped leaves that could cause an injury. *Y. filamentosa* is a stemless species that makes a dense clump of spreading and upright leaves, but the flower spike rises to about 1.5–1.8 m (5–6 ft). You can expect flowers on both species from mid- to late summer. There is a widespread belief that yuccas do not flower every year, but with an established clump which is producing new offsets, you can confidently expect some flowers every year. There is a variegated variety of both species.

It is worth trying to include plenty of fragrant shrubs such as roses, which you can enjoy even in the dark.

This view of the same rose garden shows the impact of just a few well-placed lamps, even in a large area.

Yuccas do not generally look their best planted among other shrubs in a border. Treat them as isolated specimens, or alternatively plant them in a gravel area with low plants around the base.

PHORMIUMS

Phormiums also have a sub-tropical appearance, and the variegated varieties are especially attractive by day. *Phormium tenax* has sword-like evergreen leaves up to 1.8 m (6 ft) or even more in length, with a distinctive flower spike that can be twice this height. This is a giant among phormiums, too large for a small garden, but there are many hybrids of smaller stature, many with more attractively coloured foliage. A good garden centre or specialist nursery will have a good selection, but for after-dark effect it is worth going for varieties that have a reasonable height if you want to make the most of their shape. Try some of the smaller hybrids in, for instance, a bed of gravel, which you can illuminate by floodlight or spotlights.

Phormiums are not dependably hardy in cold areas, but they will withstand quite cold winters once established.

PALMS

A palm will also add that extra ingredient that goes to give a garden a touch of distinction. The Chusan palm, *Trachycarpus fortunei* will grow quite well in a sheltered position in mild areas, though the leaves may be damaged if exposed to strong winds. It develops a typical single palm trunk clothed with the fibrous remains of old leaves, topped with new fan-like leaves. Long-established trees will flower, and a spotlight focused on the head of flowers among the palm leaves will give your garden a real touch of one-upmanship.

Cordyline australis is not a palm, but it has a similar distinctive profile. In a mild climate, it usually forms a single trunk crowned by a mass of sword-shaped leaves. This is not a plant to try in cold areas, but once established it will tolerate a reasonably cold winter. It tends to do best in coastal areas where the winters are usually less harsh.

Like the Chusan palm, *Cordyline australis* will take a few years to reach a respectable size, but for a few years until it becomes too large it makes a good candidate for a large tub. However the container will need some winter protection, as a totally frozen rootball will probably finish off a young plant. Try putting it in a cool conservatory for the winter.

SHRUBS

Although spiky plants are particularly useful where a strong profile is needed, too many will spoil the effect. Try to include a few shrubs that have very bold foliage but are not spiky. One of the most useful, because it grows fairly quickly and easily, is the false castor-oil plant (*Fatsia japonica*). It's worth growing just for its large, dark green, hand-like leaves, but it is particularly useful for its bold distinctive shape. In suitably mild areas it will grow quite large (over 2.4 m/8 ft) with ball-like clusters of white flowers in late autumn. In cold areas you will need to plant it against a sunny, sheltered wall. If you have a conservatory, grow it in a large tub or pot so that you can take it indoors to enjoy as a conservatory foliage plant for the winter.

There are some shapely plants that die down for the winter, but are none the less useful for the summer months. Where there is a large pond or an area of boggy ground, the giant 'rhubarb', *Gunnera manicata* takes some beating for sheer presence. Its huge leaves immediately command attention, making it a dramatic plant by day or night, when it can be illuminated.

Useful for a gravel area, or a bed with herbaceous plants, are the grey-leaved Scotch thistle (*Onopordum acanthium*) and the mullein *Verbascum* × *bombyciferum*. Both are easily grown as biennials but may live for longer. The Scotch thistle is a rather angular plant, growing to about 1.8 m (6 ft), the mullein has large felted leaves more than 30 cm (1 ft) long, and a grey poker-like spike growing up to around 1.8 m (6 ft), with yellow flowers. With both plants the shape and distinctive grey foliage are the attraction rather than the flowers.

GRASSES

Some of the large grasses can be particularly striking, but they need careful placing as anything as large as the pampas grass can look out of place among other border plants. Try the more vigorous types as specimens in the lawn, perhaps where they can make a focal point from the patio. Away from the clutter of other border plants they will also make a more striking silhouette against the evening sky.

Where you have space, the pampas grass (*Cortaderia selloana*) will command attention with its long-lasting tall white plumes in autumn, reaching 1.8 m (6 ft) and more. It can eventually make a huge clump. Although less dramatic against the skyline, the more compact 'Pumila' is another good candidate for illumination. A slight breeze will keep the plumes moving as they capture the light.

Among other good stately grasses to consider, one of the best is *Miscanthus sinensis*. The variety 'Silver Feather' makes a splendid autumn display with plumes over 1.8 m (6 ft) tall. There are variegated forms too, which you may want to try in order to bring more interest during the daylight hours.

Bamboos tend not to provide such good silhouettes, often forming a rather dense thicket rather than an attractive profile, but they do illuminate well and the taller ones will form a useful screen.

BORDER PLANTS

Some of the herbaceous perennial border plants can provide quite a dramatic view in failing light, or picked out in light against a dark background.

Hostas are particularly versatile, growing happily in sun or shade, and making bold foliage plants even as ground cover, without being invasive. Most of the many species and varieties make useful front-of-border plants, and are ideal for small patio beds where the leaves can cascade over the edge of the paving to soften it. For a really impressive single group to highlight in a corner of the patio, try one of the varieties with large blue-green leaves such as *H. sieboldiana* 'Elegans'.

Acanthus spinosus (bear's breeches) is a statuesque plant with large, thistle-like leaves and bold spikes of mauve-purple and white hooded flowers. Although usually grown in a border, try a single specimen in a strategic position, perhaps in a corner of the patio.

Crambe cordifolia is a distinctive plant to use where you need something big and to provide contrast against an otherwise dull background – perhaps a tall green hedge. The leaves are large, but it's the mass of smallish white flowers in sprays 1.8 m (6 ft) high or more in summer that makes it worth planting.

Red hot pokers (kniphofias) always make an arresting display. For real impact, choose tall varieties with big, bold, orange or yellow spikes. It is well worth growing several varieties, as some flower in early summer, others in late autumn. Use them in the border, but never be afraid to use them as isolated specimens, perhaps by the edge of a path, or in a patio bed where you need a plant with height and stature.

A large clump of kniphofias will be striking by day or at dusk, and at night with a spotlight on them the flower spikes – the orange 'pokers' – really will glow.

There are not many herbaceous plants that combine height with an interesting shape or outline, but *Rheum palmatum* 'Atropurpureum' is one of them. The big palmate leaves are especially colourful in spring when they are flushed purple. In summer a tall leafy spike will rise to about 1.8 m (6 ft) or more, unfurling sprays of small white flowers. It will need plenty of room, but can be useful in a border that needs height.

Arum lilies (*Zantedeschia aethiopica*) will give the patio a touch of the exotic, the large white spathes showing up against the dark green leaves in the fading light. Plant them in a corner that needs 'lifting', either planted out in the soil or in a container that you can take into a conservatory or cool greenhouse for the winter. Arum lilies need a sheltered spot in mild areas to do well, but they will be perfectly happy in pots that you can protect for the winter. 'Crowborough' is one of the best varieties for growing outdoors.

Areas that can be rather uninspiring during the day can take on a special quality after dark (see photograph opposite).

You would not give this area special thought during the day, but illuminated it becomes charming and romantic.

Very like a small arum lily is the aquatic bog arum (*Calla palustris*). Try it in a patio pond, perhaps surrounding a tasteful statue or ornament. Its creeping habit also makes it an excellent plant for the edge of the pond, helping to mask any hard lines. The flowers are like small versions of the 'calla' lilies of Easter.

FERNS

Ferns are a generally neglected group of plants, frequently regarded as rather dull background plants that lack colour. However, they have much to offer for those rather shady, perhaps damp, spots that other plants cannot tolerate well.

The beauty of most ferns lies in their shape and outline. There are plenty of ferns that have finely divided or curled fronds, but for the evening garden you will be looking for bold outline rather than fine detail, and one of the best is *Matteuccia struthiopteris*. It is popularly called the shuttlecock fern, because it forms a tall rosette of narrow upright, feathery fronds that look amazingly like a giant shuttlecock. From the moment its delicate pale green fronds unfurl and reach skywards in spring, right through to the end of the season, this plant – with such an attractive common name but lumbered with a completely offputting Latin name – will play its role as an invaluable feature plant. It will look good during the day, but at night it can be especially attractive viewed against low backlighting or illuminated from above with a spotlight.

CONTAINERS

Plants in containers have a special impact on the patio, but both containers and plants need to be big and bold if they are to attract in poor light.

If you have a conservatory or cool greenhouse in which you can overwinter the plants, there are plenty of really striking plants to grow.

The daturas are among the most magnificent, with huge hanging bells on large leafy plants — those with white flowers, such as *D. cornigera*, are the best to grow for the evening garden. The 15 cm (6 in) long pendulous white to cream flowers also have a heavy fragrance. 'Knightii' is a semi-double form. In good conditions it can grow big — 1.8 m (6 ft) high and almost as much across — and you can expect flowers from early to late summer. A combination that guarantees attention.

In some very mild areas the imposing *Agave americana* 'Marginata', with its big rosette of yellow-edged sword-like succulent leaves, will overwinter outside, but really it needs to be taken into a frost-free greenhouse or conservatory for the winter. The plant will look interesting but not especially imposing for the first year, but with age it can make an imposing specimen more than 1 m (3 ft) tall and across – a sure talking point with your visitors!

If you have to depend on frost-hardy plants there is no need for them to be dull or uninteresting. Camellias make superb evergreen tub plants, but they flower before the summer evenings come. Better to choose shrubs that flower in summer or early autumn – and the bigger or showier the blooms, the more suitable they will be for evening when colour and delicacy are quickly lost. Hydrangeas are easy and dependable. Choose the mophead or lacecap types to grow in tubs, as these have big, bold flower-heads on bushy but compact plants. There are plenty of varieties, usually in shades of blue or pink; the pink ones will show up better in failing light, but bear in mind that the soil has an effect on flower colour. Blue varieties tend to be pink unless the soil is acid. The soil may be made acid by using an ericaceous compost in a container with plenty of peat. Hydrangeas are not a good choice, however, if you tend to neglect watering.

The false castor oil plant (*Fatsia japonica*) is big and bold, with hand-shaped leaves that are attractive enough for the plant to be grown indoors as a foliage houseplant. It has a rather exotic and tender appearance despite its size, yet is hardy and dependable in moderately cold areas. It will grow to more than 1.8 m (6 ft) given time and a large enough container, and being evergreen it can be usefully used to screen an area that is not especially attractive. On mature plants you can expect candelabra ball-shaped heads of small white flowers in autumn. Use it in a sheltered spot where you need a touch of lush foliage. Picked out in light it will give the patio a lush, warm climate atmosphere. Although lacking brilliant colouring, its size and shape compensate for this.

Japanese maples (*Acer palmatum* and its various varieties, including those with finely divided and purple leaves) are not the easiest shrubs to grow, but it may be well worth trying to include some if you can find the right sheltered spot for them. It isn't necessarily the cold winters that do the most harm (though those in containers are vulnerable unless given winter protection), rather the cold winds and morning sun that can do the damage. Sometimes the leaves are wind burned, making them turn brown and shrivel, just as they begin to unfurl.

The beauty of these shrubs, quite apart from their coloured or feathery foliage, is that distinctive, angular and almost layered shape typical of Japanese maples. Grow them in tubs on the patio or perhaps in a sheltered corner of the garden that needs a focal point, but be patient as they are slow-growers.

Don't confine all your Japanese maples to tubs. They also look superb in association with water. Choose some of the green or yellow-leaved forms to grow by the edge of a pond, where their shape and colour can be reflected in the water.

Lilies are surprisingly good container plants. They need a generous, deep container, and discreet staking may be necessary, but they are undisputably arresting in flowers, and many of them are deliciously fragrant too.

Trees

Too many large trees will detract from the evening garden rather than enhance it. Trees are invaluable for creating additional height to a garden, and in the right place they can provide focal points or act as useful screens if the outlook is not particularly attractive. But in the wrong position they can also shut out the twilight and make the garden prematurely dark. They will cast deep shadows and, at worst, may block out that stunning sunset or full moon.

Try to confine most large trees to other parts of the garden, and use mainly small trees in the area set aside for evening use. If you have to use trees on the sunset side of the garden, try to choose those with a distinctive outline.

One of the best is the contorted willow (*Salix matsudana* 'Tortuosa'), which has a tracery of twisted and contorted branches that are interesting unclothed throughout the winter; in summer zig-zagging branches are still clearly visible because the narrow leaves are small enough not to mask the distinctive profile.

The corkscrew hazel (*Corylus avellana* 'Contorta') also has twisted branches that look superb against a winter sunset, and the plant is perhaps at its best in early spring when covered with hanging yellow catkins before the leaves appear. The summer foliage is itself somewhat distorted, and large enough to hide most of the branches, so it may not be such a good year-round choice.

Where a quick-growing ultimately modest-sized tree is required for a lawn specimen, the stag's-horn sumach (*Rhus typhina*) is a good choice. It makes a small tree or large shrub with sparse, wide-spreading branches that give it an open, flat-topped appearance that prevents it ever looking oppressive. The large, divided leaves are attractive all summer, but are especially beautiful in autumn as they turn shades of orange, red, yellow, and purple. On some plants the crimson cones of the fruits give a final fling at the end of the year.

Eucalypts

The eucalypts are not for very small gardens, but where there's space for a quick-growing tree, some of

Low-level lighting focuses attention within the garden, and can be especially effective in a small area.

It is always worth illuminating steps for safety reasons, but you can sometimes make a feature of them too.

the eucalyptus species are well worth including. They grow large and, although evergreen, never seem to be as oppressive as, say, a large conifer. However, you should not expect the young rounded juvenile foliage unless you coppice the plant by cutting it down every year ot two and treating it rather like a large shrub. The foliage on a large specimen is likely to be more sickle-shaped, but still with that pungent eucalyptus oil smell. In favourable areas a surprising range of eucalyptus species will survive quite cool winters; sometimes the foliage may be killed, but often the trees sprout again in spring. Among the hardiest and most dependable are *E. dalrympleana* and *E. gunnii.*

Eucalypts can be striking if floodlit, with their pale trunks and greyish leaves reflecting the light more effectively than most green-leaved trees.

FRAGRANCE

Welcome though fragrance is at any time, it is a vital ingredient of a successful evening garden. The olfactory senses become sharpened, helping to compensate for the lack of visual stimulus, and fragrances assume a special role. The still evening air on a warm summer's evening has that special smell that is at once comforting and relaxing. Even fragrances carried from the plants in gardens around you create a 'summer evening' fragrance that simply makes one feel good. A bed of night-scented stocks (*Matthiola bicornis*) can sometimes be detected several houses away as you walk along the road.

As with most good things, there are potential drawbacks. Fragrance can be overdone. A whole bed or border of different strongly aromatic plants can be overpowering, with one perfume destroying the effect of the next.

The secret is to use plenty of fragrant plants dotted around the garden, but not actually next to each other. If you want lots of variety, use more plants with delicate fragrances that will not carry so far, or plant more with aromatic foliage where the smell is released only

if crushed or brushed against, such as lemon balm (*Melissa officinalis*).

Plant annuals such as mignonette, night-scented stocks and nicotiana, in masses by the door or along a path leading to your evening garden. Their fragrance will welcome visitors and immediately help to put them in the mood for a relaxing evening.

The right fragrance

It is always difficult to classify and describe fragrances, and also unwise to be dogmatic with particular recommendations. A fragrance that one person finds attractive, another may dislike; a fragrance that one person describes as weak, another may define as strong. Trials have shown that with some plants, as many gardeners may be unsure of or dislike a particular fragrance as actually like the smell. If you only have to please yourself, try to smell before you buy. Some of the best places where you can indulge in smelling lots of fragrant plants are gardens for the blind. In the UK, for your nearest centre, try contacting the Royal National Institute for the Blind, 224 Great Portland Street, London W1N 6AA.

Fragrant flowers are best in a warm, sheltered position as the vapour from the volatile oils is more likely to be released in warm air, but are quickly dissipated by the wind. Much of the effect of any delicate fragrances will be lost in an exposed position. A patio, where there is perhaps the protection of a sunny wall and maybe screens at least at the sides, provides an ideal setting for fragrant plants, but you should not overlook other parts of the garden, where protection is provided by other shrubs and hedges.

If you do need fragrance in a fairly open position, try massed fragrant annuals or perhaps a bed of fragrant roses, so that you are not depending on a single plant for the effect. Also, make a point of using some fragrant plants at key points around the garden: by the door, beneath or around a window, and of course behind or next to a garden seat.

Raised beds, perhaps on the patio, provide a platform for many of the smaller fragrant plants that might otherwise be overlooked because the flowers have to be that much nearer nose level for the scent to be appreciated.

If your evening garden contains a shrub or mixed border, make sure there are plenty of fragrant flowers that will give a succession of olfactory delights as you walk along. Despite the earlier advice not to use very fragrant plants too close to each other, this only applies to plants in flower at the same time. Most shrubs flower for a relatively short period, and you may be able to plant a number of scented shrubs quite close to each other that flower at different times, thereby giving a variety of fragrances over a longer season. Plants with aromatic foliage can be safely planted in front, along the border, as these usually release their aroma only after a shower or other physical contact.

A scented border should be planned on the windward side of your garden, so that you and not your neighbour get the benefit of the perfume.

If you have to provide a screen, that too can be fragrant. The flowers on rose or *Philadelphus coronarius* hedges will be delicately fragrant, albeit rather short in season. Foliage hedges and screens such as *Cupressus macrocarpa* and *Thuja occidentalis* have a distinctive smell, especially if brushed against or crushed.

One of the best fragrant screens is a trellis variety of *Lonicera periclymenum*, as these are among the most fragrant honeysuckles. If you have space, plant both 'Belgica' (flowers late spring and early summer) and 'Serotina' (continues from mid summer to early autumn). Honeysuckles are usually at their most fragrant in the evening.

Fragrant climbers, including roses, can be used over arches and pergolas, but if you're not careful with the pruning some will produce most of the flowers at a height where much of the fragrance will be lost.

FRAGRANT BEDDING PLANTS

It is always worth using plenty of bedding plants. They bring colour over a long period for most of the summer, and make a garden look especially bright during the day. By incorporating plenty of fragrant types the bedding can still have a powerful impact after dark. The plants listed below are all readily available as seed, though you may find it difficult to find some of them sold as plants.

Alyssum maritimum (sweet alyssum)
This ubiquitous edging plant appears in most bedding schemes. It is often described in catalogues as fragrant, but this is easily missed unless it is massed in a drift, or in a raised bed. It is also likely to be strongest in the midday warmth, so don't expect too much in the way of evening fragrance. It is worth growing, however, as the white varieties show up well as light begins to fade towards the end of the day.

Dianthus barbatus (sweet William)
This is actually a biennial plant that you plant the previous summer, but it is so fragrant that it is well worth trying to incorporate. It finishes flowering before most other bedding plants have got into their stride and you may be able to replant with late bedding plants to follow on. There are annual varieties that can be raised like normal bedding plants, but these do not give such a good show or as much fragrance.

Dianthus heddewigii and hybrids
The annual dianthus varieties and hybrids can make colourful bedding plants, but many of them lack a strong fragrance. Check the catalogue and choose those that are fragrant.

Iberis umbellata (candytuft)
A hardy annual that will do best sown where it will flower. Bright, long-flowering, and very easy. Best in a mass or bold drift — both visually and from the fragrance viewpoint.

Matthiola (stocks)
The day-flowering stock, which are those most commonly used for bedding, are wonderfully fragrant. Unfortunately they generally have a shorter flowering period than many bedding plants, so don't devote too much space to them.

Matthiola bicornis (night-scented stock)
This is a 'must' for the evening garden. It is a hardy annual that you should sow where it will flower. During the day,

This shows how effective low-voltage lighting systems can be – the effect can be prettier than floodlighting the whole area.

You will get much more use from your conservatory by installing suitable lighting, and it will look good too.

when the flowers close, it certainly cannot be described as attractive, but find somewhere to grow a patch of it because it has one of the strongest evening fragrances.

Nicotiana (tobacco plant)
Most of the modern varieties that have been bred for their compact habit and upward-facing flowers lack scent. It's the taller varieties (such as 'Evening Fragrance') that are the most fragrant – and reach their peak performance in the evening. Some of the evening flowering fragrant nicotianas generally close during the day, but varieties such as 'Sensation Mixed' are both very fragrant and have flowers that remain open during the day. After night-scented stocks, these should be high on your list.

Lathyrus odoratus (sweet pea)
Most patios have an area where a few climbers can be used (alternatively simply grow them up 'wigwams' of canes), and sweet peas are obvious candidates. Some varieties are much more fragrant than others, so check the catalogues.

FRAGRANT SHRUBS
There are plenty of fragrant shrubs from which to choose, and those in the list below are just a shortlist of some of the most fragrant summer-flowering shrubs that you should be able to buy easily.

Buddleia davidii (butterfly bush)
This can be rather sprawling and untidy for a small area, but try to include it in the shrub border (if only for the butterflies that it will attract during the day).

Choisya ternata
Not suitable for cold areas, but otherwise a wonderful shrub. Evergreen, glossy leaves and fragrant white flowers in spring and from time to time through the summer.

Clerodendrum trichotomum
A large, late-flowering shrub that will make a good specimen plant in the lawn.

Cytisus battandieri
An excellent choice for a warm wall. Yellow flowers with a strong pineapple scent in early summer.

Lonicera periclymenum (honeysuckle)
Perhaps the best climber to choose. Whether you grow the early-flowering 'Belgica' or the late-flowering 'Serotina' you can't fail to be impressed by the power of the scent.

Lavandula (lavender)
Both flower and foliage are fragrant, and as most of the varieties are small and compact it is almost always possible to find space for a few plants. Grow isolated plants at the front of the border, or on the patio in growing areas between the paving, but better still try to find room to grow a low decorative hedge of lavender.

Philadelphus hybrids and varieties (mock orange)
Fairly large shrubs with very fragrant white flowers.

Roses
There are so many good roses, including climbers and shrub roses, that you will be spoilt for choice. Consult catalogues if you need to, but if possible see and smell them for yourself in rose gardens.

Spartium junceum (Spanish broom)
A large shrub with fragrant yellow flowers in summer.

5

PARTY EVENING

The point of having an evening garden is to *use* it. To be able to enjoy those extra few hours of pleasure each evening whenever there is fine weather, to use it as a place for relaxation and an extension of the home. And like the home it should be a place to share and entertain in.

There will be days when you simply want to relax in the stillness of a warm summer's evening, but the chances are there will be times too when you will want to share the pleasures of an evening garden with your friends – whether it's a full blown party or simply a few friends round for an evening drink, or perhaps a modest barbecue.

A successful evening party in the garden depends partly on the atmosphere created by the lighting and setting, and partly on the food and drink. The good company is taken for granted.

LIGHTING

If your aim is for a sophisticated party, keep the lighting tasteful – that usually means plain and dramatic rather than garish and colourful. The normal garden and patio lights will probably be enough, though this is the time when parasol lights come into their own, fitted to a patio set parasol. They highlight the food or place settings, and make it easy for the guests to see what they are choosing or eating. Supplementary patio lighting may also be necessary, particularly if you have more than a few guests ... nobody should have to

disappear into pools of darkness. There are plenty of free-standing patio lights with a built-in stand that you can bring out for the occasion. These won't look elegant with trailing wires cluttering up the patio during the day, but they are excellent for the occasion.

Party lights

If it is more of a fun occasion with a strong party atmosphere, there are more jolly ways to light up the occasion. Party lights (sometimes called string or festoon lights) have coloured lamps spaced along the cable (Fig. 10), that should be long enough to take through a window to a power supply indoors. The fittings will be waterproof, but you must replace any bulbs with a similar type suitable for outdoor use. Ordinary light bulbs, once hot, may shatter if splashed by cold water such as rain.

Lights of this kind can be left outdoors, and some people like to string them along a hedge, drape them along the edge of the house, or even through a suitable tree (they come in useful for festive occasions such as Christmas, when some people like to decorate an outdoor tree rather in the manner of a giant illuminated Christmas tree).

If the lead is not long enough, don't try to use an ordinary connection outdoors. You can buy special waterproof cable connectors from good specialist electrical shops and sometimes from garden centres that sell equipment for ponds.

Parasol lights are easy to fix to most patio table parasols ... and can contribute to a romantic evening.

Patio lights can be brought out for the occasion, to help you get the most from those warm summer evenings.

Fig. 10 Party lights are inexpensive, easy to put up for the occasion, and do not require permanent wiring. Although primarily decorative, they are still a useful source of light.

Patio lamps

Small, coloured, oil-filled patio lamps are available, and these are likely to be popular with children's parties as they produce a localized, sometimes flickering pool of light that can look a little spooky on a dark night. They are not much use for providing light to see by, but they add plenty of 'atmosphere'. Some of them have a metal cup that fits around the small flame so that if the lamp gets knocked over the flame is extinguished.

Candles

Patio candles have similar merits and drawbacks, perhaps not making a serious contribution to illumination, but they will provide a distinctly festive atmosphere. Some of them are perfumed, and many contain a fragrance that is supposed to keep insects at bay – a useful attribute as midges and moths have a habit of

wanting to share an evening party. Candles are fun things, and not really expensive if you consider their contribution to a party atmosphere. They can be especially useful as table decorations while you are sitting down to a meal; many of them are made as decorative lanterns; sometimes they are in the form of wax-filled glasses. However they're packaged, the flickering naked flame has romantic connotations.

Flares

Flares give off more light and the bigger flame often appeals more to children. There are lots of shapes and colours, but the chances are there will be a long cane that you can push into the ground. Burning time varies with the make and type, but you should expect at least several hours.

BARBECUES

If there is one smell that can be more stimulating than the fragrance of the flowers, it's the drifting aroma of food being cooked on a barbecue. Add the two together and you have the makings of a perfect evening.

The sounds and smells of outdoor cooking help to whet the appetite, and it adds another dimension to the evening outdoors. Food always seems to have a richer, fuller taste cooked in the open air over glowing charcoal. Even the humble sausage can become a gastronomic delight when filled with the flavour of smouldering charcoal.

Getting the charcoal to burn and raising the temperature ready for cooking can be fun or a frustration, depending on your attitude to these things (certainly you need to allow plenty of time). If it's just not your scene, you can spend your way out of the problem. There are bottled gas barbecues that will light at the turn of a switch – and those that use artificial 'coals' won't lack visual appeal either.

Choosing a barbecue

If you want your parties to appear really sophisticated, a built-in barbecue (Fig. 11) will look good and give the impression that you're an 'old hand'. You can have just as much fun, however, with something simpler and probably a lot less expensive.

Fig. 11 A built-in or permanent barbecue is worth considering if you use your garden regularly for outdoor living – and you can make it an integrated part of the garden design.

Hibachis

The simplest of all are the hibachis (Fig. 12a), which comprise a tray (or firebox) with a grill above for the food. The speed of cooking is usually controlled by a vent at the bottom of the tray, which will speed up or slow down the rate of burning. A small, single hibachi may be adequate if you simply want to cook a cosy meal for two, but you will need one of the double or triple hibachis if you're going in for entertaining. These are simply larger versions with two or three separate grills over the one base, each with its own handle.

Hibachis are inexpensive, cook the food perfectly well, and are a good introduction into barbecue cooking, so don't dismiss them. You will, however, need a firm surface, preferably with a brick or paving slab top, on which to use them. It is unwise simply to place them on a flimsy table.

Grill barbecues (Fig. 12b)

Grill barbecues have a firebox and grill rack surrounded by a metal windshield (which helps to conserve the heat). There are plenty of designs, some with a round grill, others rectangular – both cook well, so the choice is really up to you. Of course size will be dictated by the number of people you expect to entertain.

You should be able to adjust the height of the grill easily (it's likely to slide into slots in the metal windshield). This useful feature helps to control cooking time.

Some models have powered spit rods, and many of the others have the option of a manually turned spit. You can manage without these aids, but they do make cooking that much easier.

Even the simple grill barbecues usually have stout legs, but there are wheeled models (sometimes called wagon barbecues (Fig. 12c), often with additional shelf space, that have the merit of being more portable. Being able to move the barbecue easily is not only convenient for putting it away after use, it also can be very useful to be able to move it during cooking if the wind changes, or if it starts to rain and you need to move to a more sheltered position.

Kettle grills (Fig. 12d)

Kettle grills have a domed lid that can be used to cover the cooking food. This enables higher temperatures to be achieved, so that the food can cook more quickly.

D-I-Y

If you're keen on d-i-y, and would like to build yourself a barbecue, there are plenty of good kits on the market – usually you simply have to provide the bricks or

On a patio make the most of colourful containers and feature plants. The shadows add a touch of drama.

In a large garden, try to spotlight one or two key focal points, which can be very dramatic.

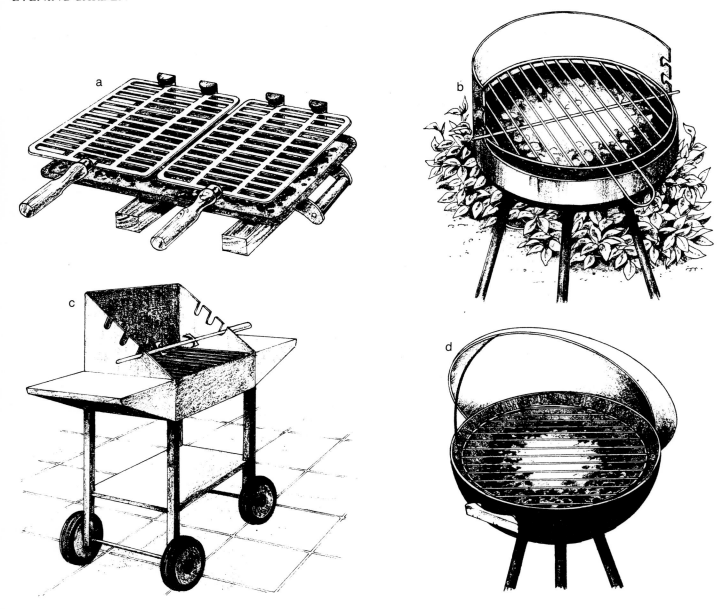

Fig. 12 Barbecues can be inexpensive or costly, but even a cheap one will cook a meal successfully. The simplest kind is the hibachi (*a*); grill barbecues (*b*) are popular, and some of them, known as trolley barbecues (*c*), have wheels and space for utensils. Kettle barbecues (*d*) have lids that can increase cooking speed.

blocks and mortar. With kits you can usually build the barbecue into a specific space, and you have lots of scope for individual design. Provided you are a reasonably competent character, there are plenty of possibilities for building a structure with doors and shelves, and plenty of space for serving too.

PREPARING A BARBECUE

Gas (usually liquefied petroleum – LPG) and electric barbecues heat reusable ceramic lava rocks, and these cook just like charcoal. As the radiant heat from the rocks vaporizes the fat you will find that the food still has that distinctive barbecue flavour.

Charcoal is the traditional fuel, available in lumps or as brickettes. Handling it is almost inevitably a messy job but, like starting a camp fire, it's all part of the fun.

Spread the charcoal in a thin layer over the firebox, extending it an inch or so beyond the grill area. Getting it to ignite is not easy without one of the lighting aids, although some charcoals are already treated for easy ignition. Otherwise, try using special lighting fuel sold for the job, or one of the other aids such as a paste that you can smear over the charcoal. Don't use anything very inflammable such as petrol or paraffin to start the barbecue, as these are potentially very dangerous … and they can affect the flavour of the food. Firelighters can be used, but use them very sparingly otherwise these too will taint the food.

Light the barbecue at least half an hour before you need to start cooking, so that the food cooks quickly once you are ready to start. Don't forget that although the charcoal will probably be glowing red at night, in daylight the surface will appear grey. Smoke, sparks and flare-ups are no part of a well-managed barbecue!

The charcoal will burn from the bottom upwards, therefore low ventilation is important. If you buy a proprietary barbecue there will be adequate ventilation, but a breeze in the right direction will usually get it burning more quickly. Some may have a damper to control the rate of burn: you will need it open at first to get the charcoal burning well, but close it to control the burn once it's well alight.

Once the charcoal is burning evenly, spread it out a bit and add more charcoal if necessary. There is no need to pile on a lot of charcoal. For normal grilling it is best to have a shallow spread of charcoal over the whole cooking area. However, if you are spit cooking it may be best to pile the fire deeper (to say 8 cm/3 in) behind the spit and extending just beneath it.

If you need to reduce the temperature while cooking, spread out the fuel. If you need more heat, flick the white ash from the surface of the charcoal.

Maintain the fire by adding fuel to the edges rather than piling more charcoal on top.

It is no use pretending that barbecue cooking is an exact business. If the weather is cold, the heat will probably be less and the food will take that much longer to cook, and of course a lot depends on how close the food is to the fire.

As a very rough indication of the heat of the fire in cooking terms, try holding your hand over the fire in the position that the food will be (but do it with care). If you have to pull your hand away immediately, it's very hot. A count of two indicates hot, three is medium-hot, down to low at five.

RECIPES FOR A SUCCESSFUL EVENING

Successful parties are never made to a set recipe – some may want to include a barbecue meal; others will find it easier to prepare a simple buffet in advance so that the evening can be spent talking to the guests rather than cooking (and getting the timing right can be a stressful experience if you're not used to coping with a barbecue). If you prefer, why not try a combination of some barbecued food along with buffet snacks?

There is no reason why you should not have a

Fennel and a yucca in a gravel bed, highlighted with a single spotlight. Choose plants with an interesting profile.

Even small plants like hostas are suitable for spotlighting because they have a striking outline. Try to hide the lamp.

normal evening meal in the garden, perhaps cooking the same food as you would for a dinner party. Just treat your garden as another room for the evening. However, meals of that kind are beyond the scope of this book. Instead the recipes below are intended as a basis upon which to build your own forumula for outdoor cooking and entertaining.

BARBECUE MEALS

Unless you are simply planning a light snack, it is a good idea to make sure you have several courses. There can be a long interval while the main barbecue meal is being prepared, and a first course will stop the interest flagging, as well as keep the hunger pangs at bay.

Keep the first course simple. Your guests only need something to nibble at while they enjoy a long, cool drink. Potato crisps and salted peanuts will keep children happy. Adults may prefer dips with raw vegetables for dunking, or paté with crispbreads. Alternatively, if there is a slight chill in the air, soup may be welcome.

The main course should include fish or meat. Children may appreciate sausages and burgers more than sophisticated meat or fish dishes, but you can use steaks, or go for salmon if you want to appeal to more developed palates. The dishes suggested in this chapter are fairly basic ones that should appeal to a wide range of tastes.

Nobody wants a plate full of vegetables on an occasion like this, and the whole atmosphere can be spoilt anyway if you have to serve up a pile of cooked veg from the kitchen.

Go for a green tomato salad, perhaps with crisps. If something more filling is required, baked potatoes are a good standby. Sauces give an extra touch of flavour to barbecue meals. You can make your own, but if you want to keep it simple, don't be afraid to try some of the ready-made barbecue sauces and relishes.

Bread never sounds an exciting part of a party menu, but it is nevertheless an invaluable element – a useful filler for anyone still hungry, and very convenient for mopping up meat juices and sauces!

Keep the sweet course simple – it needs to be something ready prepared so that you have time to enjoy the evening with your guests. Cheese and biscuits or fresh fruit may be enough. Or you may want to have some open fruit flans, or perhaps gateaux ready to bring out. Above all, the sweet should be easy and not too messy to eat outdoors, especially if guests are moving around.

Children are usually easy to please with everyday soft drinks, and beer or cider will keep many of the adults happy. Nonetheless, a few more festive-looking drinks can be expected to make it all seem something special. A suggestion will be found on page 68.

Finally, if you're expecting lots of guests, don't be afraid to do lots of pre-cooking, otherwise there will be long, embarrassing waits for the food. Fish is not usually very satisfactory done this way, but chicken, sausages, and chops, are among the meats that can be pre-cooked and finished off on the grill.

Barbecue Spare Ribs

Ingredients for 6
1.8 kg (4 lb) pork spare ribs
1 onion, sliced
5 ml (1 tsp) cornflour
75 ml (5 tbs) water
30 ml (2 tbs) sugar
3 ml (¾ tsp) chilli sauce
1 ml (¼ tsp) salt

Prepare the ribs in advance by trimming the fat from the meat and dividing into single ribs. Place them in a saucepan with the onion and cover with water. Cover the pan and simmer for 45 minutes, then drain the ribs and leave them in a shallow dish.

Mix the remaining ingredients together, after first blending the cornflour with a little liquid so that it doesn't go lumpy. Pour the mixture over the ribs and leave it in the fridge to marinade until required.

Once the barbecue is glowing red hot, place the ribs on the barbecue grill and cook for about 20 minutes, until tender. Turn them and brush with marinade regularly during cooking.

Serve with a crisp green salad, along with a jacket potato if you think something more filling is required.

Honey Chicken

Ingredients for 4
4 chicken drumsticks
30 ml (2 tbs) soy sauce
15 ml (1 tbs) clear honey
2 ml (½ tsp) ground ginger

Trim off any excess skin from the chicken, then mix all the remaining ingredients together. Brush this mixture over the chicken.

When the barbercue is ready, place the drumsticks on the grill and cook for about 20 minutes, until the juices run clear when the meat is pierced.

Turn the meat and brush with the sauce regularly while cooking.

Serve with a green salad.

If you want a change from chicken, try portions of rabbit.

Trout with Fennel

Ingredients for 1
225 g (8 oz) trout
60 g (2 oz) butter, softened
2 ml (½ tsp) fennel seeds
Half a lemon
Salt and pepper

Gut and clean the trout and place it on a square of foil, large enough to enclose the fish loosely during cooking.

Mix together the butter and fennel seeds and place in the belly cavity of the fish. Slice the lemon and arrange along the top of the fish, then sprinkle with salt and pepper before folding the fish to form a loose parcel.

Place the foil package onto the barbecue and cook for approximately 45 minutes until the fish flakes easily from the bones.

You don't have to use trout — try mackerel or another fish of about the same weight. Fish steaks (such as cod or salmon), will require less cooking time (about 20 minutes).

Baked Potatoes

If you start early enough, all the cooking can be done on the barbecue. Scrub and dry the potatoes, rub them with a little butter, and wrap in foil. Over a medium fire, they should take about 50 minutes on the grill, unless very large. If there is not enough space for everything, you can place them around the edge of the grill, but be prepared for them to take longer (to test if they are ready, pierce with a fork or pinch with gloved fingers).

Jacket potatoes can also be cooked in the fire if grill space is limited, but it is more difficult to judge cooking times, and to achieve even cooking.

It's easier to cook them in the oven (190°C/375°F) for about 45 minutes, then wrap them in foil and keep hot with the barbecue. If you have a microwave cooker, there is of course an even smarter short-cut.

Shish Kebabs

9 kg (2 lb) lean lamb
16 rashers streaky bacon
2 onions
2 green peppers
1 red pepper
Salt and pepper
Cooking oil

Cut the lamb into 2.5 cm (1 in) cubes, and after stretching the bacon to make it thin, roll each piece of lamb in a piece of bacon.

Yuccas are a good choice because they have a strong profile and big pale flowers that show up well in poor light.

If you have a conservatory, try bringing out a colourful container-grown plant such as this *Lantana camara*.

Cut the onions and peppers into fairly large pieces, and thread the meat and vegetables onto long skewers designed for the job. Alternate between meat and pieces of onion and pepper.

Brush lightly with oil (you can then sprinkle over a herb such as rosemary if you like this), then grill. Turn the skewers frequently.

Finally, season with salt and pepper.

There are lots of variations on skewer cooking, and this kind of meal can be fun to prepare and to eat. For a first course you can use small skewers with fruit such as grapes, peaches, bananas, and pineapple, and for the main course the meat can range from pieces of sausage through leg or shoulder of lamb, pork, bacon, and ham to kidneys and chicken livers. Any firm fish, such as lobster or prawns can be used too. Apart from peppers and onions you can use small tomatoes, button mushrooms, and courgettes.

Boozy Bananas

Ingredients for 1
1 large banana
15 ml (1 tbs) rum, whisky or brandy

Place the bananas on the grill and cook until the skin turns black. Then put in serving dishes and slit the skins to pour in the alcohol.

Eat the cooked flesh out of the skin.

A SUMMER BUFFET

A barbecue is fun, but not right for every occasion. A buffet meal is less work at the time, and has the advantage of being moved indoors easily if the weather takes a turn for the worse.

Most of the food can be prepared in advance, although salad vegetables should not be done too far in advance, otherwise they will lose their crispness. And meringues should not be filled until the last minute or they will become soft.

All buffet recipes can be used for outdoor entertaining, but it makes sense to keep to dishes that can be eaten without cutlery (although it is always a good idea to have plenty of knives and forks available).

The recipes below may be enough for a small informal get-together with a couple of friends, but if you are entertaining more people, you will naturally want a greater variety of dishes, as well as a bigger quantity of food.

Herby Salmon Bites

Ingredients for about 20
120 g (4 oz) plain flour
Pinch of salt
15 ml (1 tbs) chopped fresh parsley or 5 ml (1 tsp) dried
10 ml (2 tsp) chopped fresh sage or 2 ml (½ tsp) dried
30 g (1 oz) lard
Cold water to mix

Filling
225 g (8 oz) low-fat soft cheese
1 egg, separated
1 lemon, grated rind and juice
213 g (7 oz) tin salmon, bones removed
salt and pepper
15 ml (1 tbs) mayonnaise
radishes and cucumber to garnish

Preheat the oven to 200°C (400°F), Gas No. 6.

Sieve together the flour and salt and mix in the herbs. Rub in the fat until the mixture resembles breadcrumbs and mix with a little cold water to form a firm dough.

Roll the dough out until it is approximately 12 cm (¼ in) thick. Using a small round cutter, cut circles of pastry and place on a baking sheet. Prick each pastry circle all over with a fork and bake in the preheated oven for 10–15 minutes until the pastry is golden. Leave to cool.

To make the filling, beat together the cheese, egg yolk, lemon rind and juice, salmon and seasoning. Fold in the mayonnaise. Whisk the egg white until stiff, then fold this into the cheese mixture. Place the mixture into a piping bag fitted with a star nozzle. Pipe small swirls onto the pastry bases and garnish with thin slivers of radishes and pieces of cucumber.

The pastry bases can be made the day before and stored in an airtight container. Swirl on the salmon topping just before serving.

CONSIDERING THE NEIGHBOURS

Parties that can be enjoyable for those invited can be a source of great annoyance to neighbours who simply have to put up with the noise, smoke, smell, and perhaps disturbing lights, that they feel are being thrust upon them.

Because one's perception of this kind of outdoor party can seem so different, depending on which side of the fence you're on, the easiest solution is to invite the neighbours. At the very least, it is a courtesy to warn them of your plans.

There will probably be times when you have to moderate the 'nuisance level' to consider your neighbours. It is a good idea to start off in the garden, but if the party goes on until late move indoors to finish it off.

You can do a lot to prevent lights being a nuisance at any time by looking at the direction of the beams in relation to other properties. They can almost always be redirected to avoid falling across the windows of neighbouring properties. Even if the direction cannot be changed, siting the lamps high to reflect downwards rather than low reflecting upwards may be enough.

Barbecue smells can stimulate when you are waiting to be fed, but the drift of onions and fat among the smoke can be perplexing rather than pleasurable if it is simply drifting in through a window. Try to find a site where this will not be a problem – sometimes moving the barbecue just a few feet can solve the problem.

Needless to say, barbecues should always be a sufficient distance from wooden fences anyway, so as not to present a fire hazard.

Ham Curls

120 g (4 oz) honey roast ham
225 g (8 oz) tin pineapple rings, cubed
Salt and pepper
Cocktail sticks

Cut the ham into 2.5 cm (1 in) strips. Place a chunk of pineapple on each strip and sprinkle with salt and pepper. Roll up, securing with a cocktail stick.

Beef Curls

120 g (4 oz) sliced beef
120 g (4 oz) grapes, deseeded
Cocktail sticks

Cut the beef into 2.5 cm (1 in) strips. Wrap around the grapes, securing with a cocktail stick.

St Clements Choux Bites

Ingredients for about 24
75 g (2½ oz) plain flour
Pinch of salt
60 g (2 oz) butter
140 ml (¼ pt) water
2 eggs, beaten

Filling
225 g (8 oz) low-fat soft cheese
45 ml (3 tbs) sieved icing sugar
1 lemon, grated rind and juice
1 orange, grated rind
140 ml (¼ pt) double cream, whipped
Shreds of lemon and orange rind for decoration

Preheat the oven to 200°C (400°F), Gas No. 6.

Sieve the flour and salt onto a piece of paper and put

Coloured lights tend to make foliage and flower colours look unreal – useful though if you want to create a mysterious effect.

Party time. Coloured party or string lights are fun and easy to hang for that special occasion.

it to one side. Place the butter and water in a saucepan and heat over a medium heat until the butter has melted and the water is boiling vigorously. Quickly add the flour and beat until the mixture forms a ball. Leave to cool slightly, then gradually add the eggs, beating after each addition until the mixture is of a piping consistency.

Place the choux pastry into a piping bag fitted with a plain nozzle. Pipe the mixture into small balls (about the size of a walnut) on a lightly greased baking sheet.

Place in the preheated oven and cook for 15–20 minutes until well risen and golden. Pierce each ball with a sharp knife, then leave to cool.

To make the filling, beat together the cheese, icing sugar, lemon rind and juice and orange rind. Fold in the whipped cream and pipe in this mixture into the cooled choux pastries. Arrange attractively on a serving plate and sprinkle with shredded lemon and orange rind.

Strawberry and Kiwi Nestlets

Ingredients for about 20
Meringue mixture or 20 bought meringue cases
225 g (8 oz) strawberries
225 g (8 oz) kiwi fruits
Redcurrant jelly to glaze

Either make your own meringue cases (good recipe books will tell you how to do this), or buy them to save time.

If you choose to buy the cases, you need only slice the strawberries and kiwis and lay them on the nests shortly before serving.

To glaze the strawberries, gently heat the redcurrant jelly until runny, then brush over each strawberry.

Sparkling Fruit Cup

Ingredients for 12
2 oranges, sliced
2 lemons, sliced
90 g (3 oz) grapes, black or white, deseeded
Half a pineapple, peeled and crushed
1 kiwi fruit, peeled and sliced
60 g (2 oz) castor sugar
2 bottles sparkling white wine
280 ml (½ pint) orange juice

Place all the ingredients in an attractive glass bowl and sprinkle it with the sugar.

Add the wine and orange juice before serving.

6

PRACTICAL MATTERS

Although you can enjoy an evening garden without lights, those ideal moments when light, weather, and opportunity come together, are usually fleeting. Garden lighting of some kind, whether creative and mood-setting or purely functional, will be necessary to get the best from your evening garden.

Buying garden lights isn't quite as simple as buying a desk lamp, and fixing it can sometimes be a lot more complicated. There are simple low-voltage systems (Fig. 13) with a transformer that you have in the house, with low-voltage cables running into the garden – safe, efficient and simple to install. But the power and usefulness of this kind of lamp is obviously limited, and if you want something like permanent floodlighting, it can become a job for a qualified electrician.

This is not a technical do-it-yourself wiring book, and you will need to seek professional advice if you are in any doubt about wiring garden lights.

It is, however, useful to have an idea of what might be involved. Even if you have to employ someone to do the work for you, it is usually helpful to know what they may have to do.

LOW-VOLTAGE LIGHTING

Low-voltage lights are very popular, and there are many different styles from which to choose. Never be

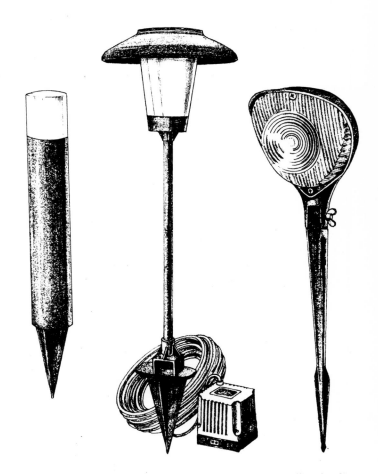

Fig. 13 Low-voltage lights like these are easy to install and safe to use. The transformer is placed indoors and only a low-voltage cable used outside.

Flares don't provide a lot of light, but they can make a tremendous contribution to an evening garden party.

Don't confine your flares to the patio. Dot them around the garden to encourage guests to explore.

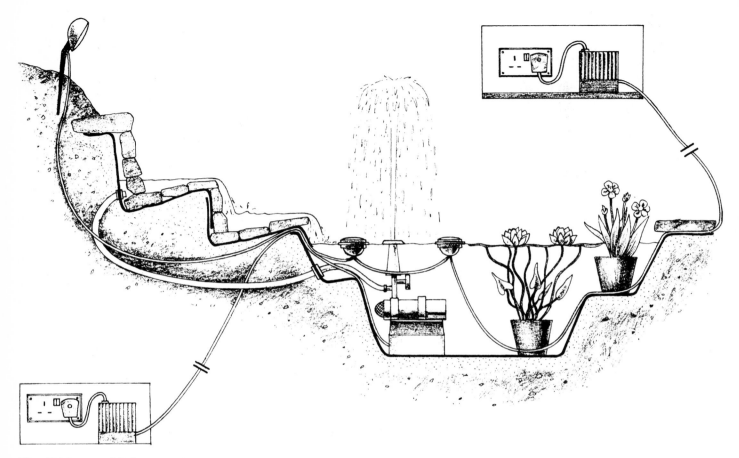

Fig. 14 Most pond lighting, and many small pumps, are run on low-voltage circuits. A transformer reduces the voltage, and these are perfectly safe even in water.

misled into thinking that low voltage means low impact. Outside, even a low-powered light seems to have lots of illuminating power.

Low-voltage lights are likely to be sold as kits, complete with transformer (Fig 14). This is located inside the house, close to a socket, and the socket switch is used as the light switch. Most of them run at 12 volts, and in some cases car light bulbs can be used as replacements.

Some of the low-voltage systems are very flexible. It is often possible to locate the lamps anywhere along the length of cable supplied, and the colour of the light can be changed by choosing different-coloured filters.

You can bury the cable like mains cable, if you want to avoid trailing wires, but one advantage of most low-voltage systems is that they can be easily moved around the garden.

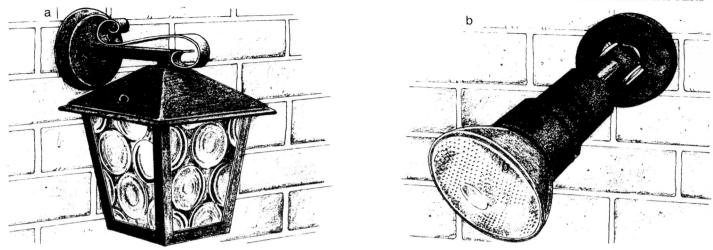

Fig. 15 It's simple to fix mains voltage lights to the house, as there should be a convenient circuit indoors. Popular wall fittings are lanterns (*a*), wall spotlights (*b*), and globes (*c*). Often you can buy matching lamps for post mounting.

MAINS LIGHTING

The simplest mains lights to install are wall-mounted lamps (Fig. 15a–c) where you can just extend the house-wiring circuit.

Outdoor bulkhead lights are functional but relatively cheap and widely available from d-i-y stores. If you want to illuminate a large drive or path by the house, they will give good coverage if mounted high enough – it's worth using an extension lead and getting a helper to hold the light in the planned position to get an idea of the light coverage. It's better to do this than go to all the trouble of fixing it to the wall before you find out that it's not exactly where you want it to be.

It will be most convenient if you can fix it in a position where you can take a spur from a power circuit socket outlet. It is possible to wire it into a lighting circuit, though the position of the cables may not be so convenient (and you need to check that more lights will not overload the lighting circuit). This is most likely to happen if you are installing powerful flood-lights (ask an electrician if you're in doubt about loadings).

Detailed fitting instructions are not given here because fittings and ratings may vary from country to country. Consult a *recent* book on electrical wiring in your local library; better still, pay an electrician to do it for you if you doubt your own knowledge and ability.

Don't expect good instructions to come with the light fitting. Occasionally they are adequate, but sometimes they are scant or non-existent.

If you do employ an electrician, you may be able to keep the cost down by doing some of the job yourself. You can drill the hole in the house wall where the light is to be fitted, using a 10 mm masonry drill long enough to go through both leaves of a cavity wall in one pass, for the cable, and drill and plug the wall to take any light fittings.

Any holes through which cables must pass should be angled slightly upwards from the outside, so that water does not run down the cable and into the hole. If you are doing the wiring yourself, seal around the baseplate of the light fitting with a non-setting mastic designed for the job (unless there is already a water-proof seal) to prevent water seeping into the fitting.

Mains spotlights and floodlights used around the garden, other than those fixed to the house wall, will really need a special power supply buried underground – you should not leave trailing mains cables that could be damaged by tools or simply tripped over. It demands careful planning. Laying underground cable is time-consuming and expensive, and it needs to be in the right place first time. It may be worth trying the lights out using an extension cable from indoors to make sure they really will meet expectations in the garden, before laying the permanent cable.

A light that is effective in one position in spring or summer could possibly be better used elsewhere in, say, autumn or winter. If you are likely to want to move your lights around, consider an outdoor lighting circuit with several outdoor sockets.

Take plenty of time working out the best and shortest route for the garden power circuit. Take into account where sockets might be useful for power tools such as hedge-trimmers and lawnmowers. Planning can be lots of fun anyway, and it is time well spent.

You need to consider obstacles such as wide concrete paths (you may be able to tunnel under a narrow one), or areas of paving, and where possible route the cable beneath a lawn rather than a flower bed (you are less likely to start digging in the lawn).

Armoured cable can be used, but you will probably find conduit a simple solution if you're doing the job yourself (plastic conduit can be joined in straight pieces or with elbows or tees, using a solvent-weld). In either case you will probably find that regulations demand a depth of at least 45 cm (18 in). Ordinary 1 mm^2 two core and earth cable will probably be adequate for fixed lights where the length of cable is not very long. If the circuit is long, 1.5 mm^2 cable may be necessary to offset the voltage drop.

If an electrician is being employed, ask for one quote where he arranges for the trench excavations, and one where you have done the labouring in advance. You may consider that it is worth doing the digging yourself.

If you install the lights yourself, double-check that fittings and any sockets are earthed properly, and that any sealing grommets are in place to keep out moisture. Remember that you must use outdoor sockets; these have a cover that protects them when they are not in use.

Don't forget that you need a switch to turn the lights on and off! You may have a switching facility in the circuit that you could use (perhaps in a residual current circuit breaker), but it is more convenient to have a switch by the back or front door – a two-way switch will enable you to turn the lights on from more than one position.

A residual current circuit breaker (it may also be called a residual current device, or an earth leakage circuit breaker) is worth having even in indoor circuits; where electricity is taken into the garden it should be considered essential. This requirement now forms part of the Wiring Regulations in countries such as Britain. An RCCB will cut off the power in a fraction of a second if a fault occurs or a cable is damaged.

Never be tempted to fix sockets or light fittings to a fence. It isn't safe.

Party or festoon lights, where the lampholders are already fixed to a length of cable to thread through a tree, along a hedge, or just around the patio or outside the house, need none of the work or expense of spotlights and the like.

If you use them for the occasional party, close to the house, the cable can simply be taken indoors through an open window. If they are to form a permanent fixture by the house, the cable will have to be taken through a hole drilled in the wall. Just plug into a socket indoors. Extension leads are usually available if needed.

Some free-standing patio lights intended for occasional use can also be treated in this way, though there is likely to be the potential hazard of a trailing cable.

BUYING LIGHTS

Simple outdoor bulkhead lights and lanterns (Figs. 16*a* and *b*) are widely available at d-i-y stores and lighting shops, and many low-voltage garden lights are readily available from garden centres, along with mains party or festoon lights. In the case of underwater lights, it is worth trying pond suppliers too.

The more elaborate outdoor lamps, such as mains spotlights and floodlights, and perhaps even lampposts, are less widely available. For these it's well worth sending away for catalogues first, then asking for local stockists. For pond lighting (Fig. 17*a* and *b*) it

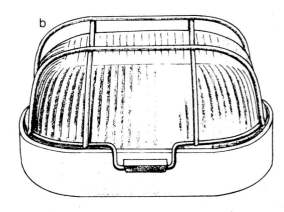

Fig. 16 Lanterns (*a*) on a pillar or low wall are welcoming and can provide useful light near a path; wall-mounted bulkhead lights (*b*) are adequate if you just want a bright light.

75

Fig. 17 Underwater lighting can bring an extra sparkle to a pond at night. Some lights will float or can be submerged (*a*); some fountains have built-in lighting (*b*).

is worth sending away for catalogues from water garden specialists.

Don't expect to be able to get all the outdoor cable and light fittings from a local electrical shop (though they may be able to order them for you). You might have to go to an electrical specialist, but be prepared that many of these are more used to dealing with tradesmen – you'll probably have to know exactly what you want; don't expect to find supermarket-type shelves for browsing. Provided you're clear about what you want, however, most specialist shops are very helpful.

APPENDIX

USEFUL ADDRESSES

The following manufacturers produce garden lighting equipment in the UK; some of the companies producing the more expensive speciality lighting equipment will also export abroad.

The companies below should be able to give you details of your nearest stockist, and in some cases they will be able to provide you with leaflets or catalogues. It is worth studying as many of these as possible before deciding on the type of lighting equipment to buy.

Sommer Allibert (UK) Ltd., Berry Hill Industrial Estate, Droitwich, Worcestershire, WR9 9AB. Tel: 0905 774221.
Mains parasol lights and standard (patio) lamps, suitable for use with their garden furniture

R. J. Chelsom & Co Ltd., Squires Gate Industrial Estate, Blackpool, Lancashire, FY4 3RN. Tel: 0253 46324.
Range of ornate mains garden lighting including cast aluminium lamp-posts and wall lamps

Delta Accessories and Domestic Switchgear Ltd., Whitegate, Broadway, Chadderton, Oldham, Lancashire, OL9 9QG.
Outdoor festoon lighting

The English Street Furniture Co., Somers House, Linkfield Corner, Redhill, Surrey, RH1 1BB. Tel: 0737 60986.
Elegant reproductions of Victorian gas lamp-posts and lanterns (electric)

Hozelock-ASL Ltd., Haddenham, Aylesbury, Bucks, HP17 8JD. Tel: 0844 291881.
Low-voltage patio/garden lights

Linolite Ltd., Malmesbury, Wiltshire, SN16 9JX. Tel: 0666 822001.
Mains wall lights

Frank Odell Ltd., 70 High Street, Teddington, Middlesex, TW11 8JD. Tel: 01–977 8158
Mains patio and party lights, garden and wall lights. Flares and candles

Philips Lighting, PO Box 298, City House, 420 London Road, Croydon, Surrey, CR9 3QR. Tel: 01–689 2166

Plug-in: Kopex International Ltd., 189 Bath Road, Slough, Berkshire, SL1 4AR. Tel: 0753 34931.
Mains and low-voltage patio and garden lights. Low-voltage pond lights. Party lights

Prices Patent Candles Ltd., 110 York Road, Battersea, London, SW11 3RU.

Ring Lighting, Gelderd Road, Leeds, LS12 6NB. Tel: 0532 791791.
Mains patio and garden lights. Wall lights. Party lights. Parasol lights

Stapeley Water Gardens Ltd., Stapeley, Nantwich, Cheshire, CW5 7LH. Tel: 0270 623868.
Mains and low-voltage party lights, mains and low-voltage pond lights

Thorn Lighting Ltd., 284 Southbury Road, Enfield, Middlesex, EN1 1TJ. Tel: 01–363 5353.
Mains garden and wall lights

Victorian Lace Ltd., 40 Solent Road, Havant, Hampshire, PO9 1JH. Tel: 0705 492816.
Modern versions of traditional ornate lamp-posts

D. W. Windsor Ltd., Pindar Road, Hoddesdon, Herts. Tel: 0992 445666.
Reproductions of Victorian and traditional lamp-posts and lamps (electric)

INDEX